Talking to Lewis and Clark

by Henry Lee

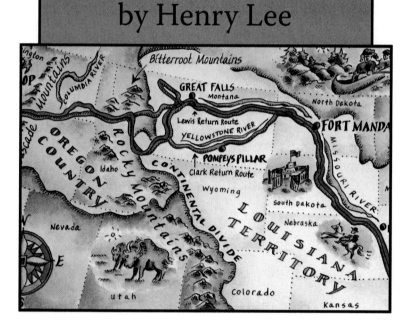

PEARSON

Glenview, Illinois • Boston, Massachusetts • Chandler, Arizona
Upper Saddle River, New Jersey

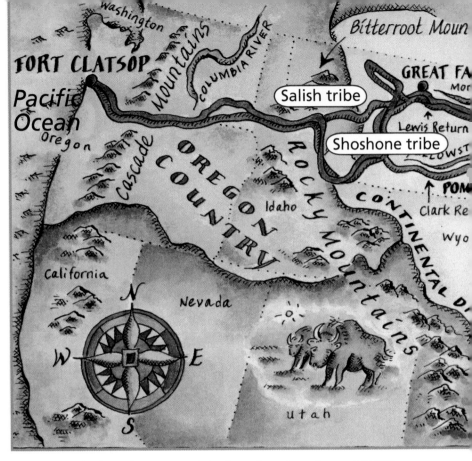

This map shows the route Meriwether Lewis and William Clark traveled. These men traveled from St. Louis (east) to Fort Clapstop (west). They explored the land by the Missouri River. Lewis and Clark met four Native American groups.

Lewis and Clark

Meriwether Lewis and William Clark were explorers. In 1803 President Thomas Jefferson asked Lewis and Clark to go on a trip. He asked them to travel to a new part of the United States. France sold the United States this large piece of land. It became known as the Louisiana Territory. The job of Lewis and Clark was to report what they discovered.

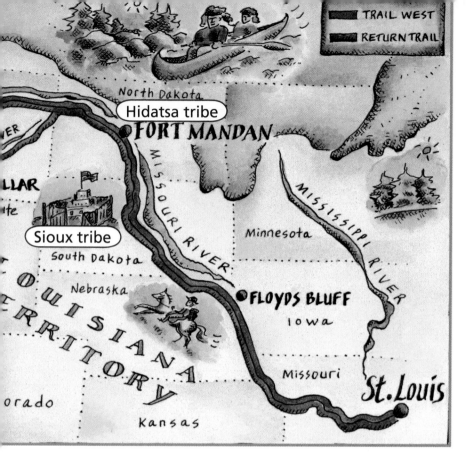

Lewis and Clark Travel West

Lewis and Clark began their journey in 1804. They started the trip with a team of people near St. Louis, Missouri. The plan was to travel west to visit places along the Missouri River. Native American people lived in these lands.

Lewis and Clark spoke only English. On the journey, they used special ways to communicate with the Native Americans.

Plains Sign Language

First, Lewis and Clark and their team crossed the Great Plains. This is where many different groups of Native American people lived. Each group had its own language.

It was hard to learn all of the different languages. This is why the Native Americans invented the Plains Sign Language. This language was easier to learn. It was a way to talk by making signs, or words, with their hands.

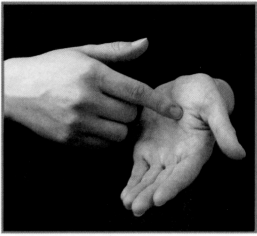

To sign *big* in Plains Sign Language, hold your hands closely together and slowly move your hands away from each other.

To sign the word *and*, hold your left hand open and touch your open palm with your right index finger.

George Drouillard

Lewis and Clark were lucky to have George Drouillard with them on the trip. George learned Plains Sign Language when he was a young boy. His mother was a Shawnee Native American.

The group traveled to the Shoshone (shuh SHOH nee) nation. Lewis wrote accounts of this part of the trip in his journal. He wrote that George knew Plains Sign Language very well. George helped Lewis and Clark communicate with the Native Americans.

---

communicate: to exchange information by writing or speaking

Lewis and Clark Get More Help

In November of 1804, Lewis and Clark met a man named Toussaint (too SANT) Charbonneau (shahr boh NOH). He was a fur trader who lived with Hidatsa Native Americans. He also spoke French. Charbonneau was married to a Shoshone Native American princess named Sacajawea.

Lewis and Clark hired Charbonneau because they thought he and Sacajawea could help on their journey. Sacajawea helped guide them through Shoshone lands. Charbonneau and Sacajawea helped Lewis and Clark find the source of the Missouri River. They also helped Lewis and Clark translate Native American languages.

---

source: place where a river begins
translate: to change from one language into another

Communication

When Lewis and Clark first met the Salish Native Americans, they could not understand each other. The Salish did not understand Plains Sign Language. Charbonneau and Sacajawea helped Lewis and Clark communicate with the Salish.

When Lewis and Clark spoke to the Salish chief, their words were translated four times. It took a long time to translate the Salish language.

The Language Chain:

1. Lewis and Clark's English words were translated into French by Francois Labiche (lah BEESH).

2. Toussaint Charbonneau translated French into Hidatsa.

3. Sacajawea translated Hidatsa into Shoshone.

4. A Shoshone boy translated Shoshone into Salish.

5. The chief spoke in Salish to the boy.

6. The boy gave the chief's answer to Sacajawea.

7. The language chain continued.

8. Lewis and Clark got their answer after four translations.